Make It

Pattern Art

Kristy Stark, M.A.Ed.

Publishing Credits

Rachelle Cracchiolo, M.S.Ed., *Publisher*
Conni Medina, M.A.Ed., *Managing Editor*
Nika Fabienke, Ed.D., *Series Developer*
June Kikuchi, *Content Director*
John Leach, *Assistant Editor*
Kevin Pham, *Graphic Designer*

TIME For Kids and the TIME For Kids logo are registered trademarks of TIME Inc. Used under license.

Image Credits: All images from iStock and/or Shutterstock.

Library of Congress Cataloging-in-Publication Data

Names: Stark, Kristy, author.
Title: Make it : pattern art / Kristy Stark, M.A.Ed.
Description: Huntington Beach, CA : Teacher Created Materials, 2018. | Audience: K to Grade 3.
Identifiers: LCCN 2017029995 (print) | LCCN 2017030559 (ebook) | ISBN 9781425853211 (eBook) | ISBN 9781425849474 (pbk.)
Subjects: LCSH: Art--Technique--Juvenile literature.
Classification: LCC N7433 (ebook) | LCC N7433 .S69 2018 (print) | DDC 700--dc23
LC record available at https://lccn.loc.gov/2017029995

Teacher Created Materials

5301 Oceanus Drive
Huntington Beach, CA 92649-1030
http://www.tcmpub.com

ISBN 978-1-4258-4947-4

© 2018 Teacher Created Materials, Inc.
Printed in China
Nordica.022018.CA21800002

We can see
patterns.
We can make art.

This is a zebra.

It has a pattern.

This is art.

It has a pattern.

This is a snake.

It has a pattern.

This is art.

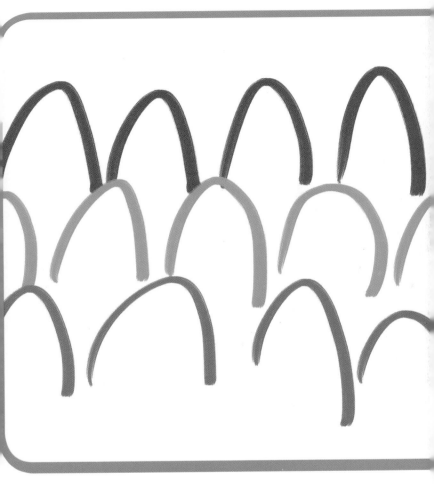

It has a pattern.

See patterns.
Make art.